The Half Turn

The Half Turn

Poems by

Aaron Lelito

© 2023 Aaron Lelito. All rights reserved.
This material may not be reproduced in any form, published,
reprinted, recorded, performed, broadcast,
rewritten or redistributed without
the explicit permission of Aaron Lelito.
All such actions are strictly prohibited by law.

Cover image and author photo by Aaron Lelito
Cover design by Shay Culligan

ISBN: 978-1-63980-393-4

Kelsay Books
502 South 1040 East, A-119
American Fork, Utah 84003
Kelsaybooks.com

Acknowledgments

Thank you to the following publications, where versions of these poems previously appeared:

Inklette Magazine: "Incremental," "So called inside" (as "Clear Night")

The Primer: "Coda"

The Purposeful Mayonnaise: "Another Anchor," "Upward Impermanence," "Ministry of Trust"

SPECTRA Poets Volume 1: "Ephemera," "Sculpting the Clay," "Grinning Ghost"

Streetcake Magazine: "Notice"

Contents

Saint Lucy	15
Cardinal and song	16
The Late Lacking of Fire	17
With One Hand Holding On	18
For Sylvie, for Ruth	20
Moon in water	21
Threshold Dweller	22
Uncertainty	24
Chatter	25
Wholeness	26
Ephemera	27
Sculpting the Clay	28
Grinning Ghost	29
Try to enter	30
Another Anchor	31
Notice	32
Ask	33
Seeking Clarity Amid Change	34
I'm Hollow	35
Incremental	36
All My Songs	37
So called inside	38
Ineffably Awake	39
Upward Impermanence	40
What I Remember	41
Unconditional Air	43
Two Winds	44
Self-Absorption	45
Our worldly winds	46
Ministry of Trust	47
To Feel Better	48
Jade	49

An improvised ritual 51
Coda 52
The Half Turn 53
The crack of expansion 55

What more glorious condition of being can we imagine than from impure to be becoming pure. It is almost desirable to be impure that we may be the subjects of this improvement. That I am innocent to myself. That I love & reverence my life! That I am better fitted for a lofty society today than I was yesterday to make my life a sacrament—What is nature without this lofty tumbling.
—Henry David Thoreau, *Journal (July 16, 1851)*

The attitude of resistance is one of weakness, inasmuch as it only faces an enemy; it has its back to all that is truly attractive.
—Henry David Thoreau, *Journal (August 30, 1856)*

Saint Lucy

It takes a sludge-green
sea to turn
the year

from the silence of Saint
Lucy to the starlight
of the leaves' lost gesture.

How gently can I search for palms
extended from paradise?

Light drifts through
auroral unrest,
where the winter sun never reaches.

Heat leaves
its requisitions among
the prowling plumes.

How purely can I gather atonement
between blossoms and dirt?

The energy of our gestures, the search
for palms, the quivering
of plumes. The containment

of something in the air that is no longer
mapped into matter. The practice
of oblivion.

How spaciously can I exchange self
for the shivering of pewter skies?

Cardinal and song,
dark attic and door

substance in solitude:
the miracle of mice

only noticed
when conditions arise—

is one miracle
enough

The Late Lacking of Fire

A separate self;
scattered branches on the ground—

transformation between
beings in their unfurling

frailty, blinking and then
looking away. In the garden

with armfuls of kindling

the fallen foliage,
as the cold air encircles us

my reticence and splayed
bark, the ashes of your

grammar, our inability
to spire in blazing

celestial crests—

We expend the only energy
left, avoiding the extremes

of heat and height,
deliberating in the darkness,

a wordless emanation
into separate selves

disentangling these limbs.

With One Hand Holding On

I let out drops
of inky offerings,
showing like tracks

trailing back to the moment
things got so off course,
at the old house

laying out clipped foliage

on the mantle
because it made me feel
connected to the trunk

and root I broke away.
I left the final flowers out,
placed in the dining room—

a centerpiece in the late style

of confession, like the deep
seed of each day's first
impulse to take sparse photos

of storefronts and blurry shapes
in other people's yards,
brick walls and fenceposts,

the parallel lines of our slow decline.

Shadowy motions within windows
are easy to imagine from memory,
framed bodies held in pose,

tensed up in painfully ordinary
arrangements, in simple kitchen talk;
yet the concession of not being there,

inside, embodied like we once were

keeps me from finding
that same street again, from finding out
that someone cut down

the old rhododendron bush
now that there's nowhere to lay out
its purple flowers—and I'm left

with one hand holding onto them.

For Sylvie, for Ruth

A train unaccompanied,
dim and drifting through
the seeming slightness:

the blower of wind
nearby enough to startle
other ghosts, to arise light

from its achromatic depths.
Thoughts bend upon
the slowness of attention,

the penciled message
folded onto itself by
sedulous hands.

Thoughts bend upon
ring and finger, the
apparitions pointing

across lakes lengthwise
and not waiting to be claimed.
They bend upon trains passing,

over nighted glass, passing
through rifts or waves,
into ambient expansion,

the moment of being
different in every way
starting now.

Moon in water—
unfolding melody
tethered
to echoes

vanishing
in breathlessness—
the tacit entry
into night air

Threshold Dweller

What's so different
tonight—

steps toward
other feet,

the porous
entry into

another person's
entirety.

What'll still be here
at dawn—

the wait can take
place in any other city

in the world, but
it still wilts within

without permission.
Rooftop bars

still shine
from the sidewalks,

piano and bass
play on—

but the violet
summits in seconds

overhead, high
as the velvet

softness of being
in the way.

Uncertainty

Uncertainty
is knowing
the fallen oak, but
not how the ground

can cradle so
gently; doubt lingers
and solidifies
in familiar

textures, in advent
of ceremonial
time. The air blurred
and circling is pure form,

the carefulness
of not cresting
too soon, the spectacle
of withdrawing

heaviness and blame;
the impossibility of
uprighting things fallen
aimless or fallow,

awaits some twist
of an unblossomed branch

Chatter

Pruning and grasping—
stuck

Bound to
dissolution—
same story

Birdsong—
in the leaves
without concept

Light touch—
start with sticks

Wholeness

when lost
is the paradox

of wholeness—
a rock in palm

a burnt match.

Ephemera

A labor of the day
to which matters
of calendar
are applied,

from which combustion occurs,
out of which smoke spirals,

like talk
to the temples,
like leaves
to the evergreens,

a truth
wasted on the proof.

An idea that remains an idea
can sit upon the stone
and float over the earthen abyss
unbound.

Sculpting the Clay

A limited self
on a day, on an any now

(A lock)

Tuning into the field,
an ambient radiance

(A key)

Sculpting the clay, inside and out
(Do what you want with it)

Photons that our eyes eat between pulses
(Do what you want with them)

Grinning Ghost

Among the marl,
the settled attention of an old arborist

who sees
an ordinary inch

as if
it was wrought with a dense mile.

The earliest
ringlets yet to be willowed;

the gleaming
approach of incandescence.

Try to enter
the park at night

Gate closed—
walk around

Notice the movement,
the daft ritual

Walk around,
enter elsewhere

Beyond limits
of perimeter

Send forth light,
weightless gaze

Another Anchor

Listen for bark
and leaf,
cardinal eyes

always scanning—

Disentangle solidity,
loosen the letters
written to the valley

and locate the apple
following fog,
falling upward,

an equivalent
of altitude,

a fruition
of abandon

Notice

(thoughts arise)

    they are   immeasurable
                                terrain

(they cause)

        mistakes in
        perception

(that cause)

        resisting
        connection

(between)

        seeing with the spotlight

(and)

        seeing with the floodlight

Ask

How to illuminate
the vacuum,
clearly empty

and yet not non-
being, like

when faces turn
to backs of heads
after the show, like

nostalgia for places
forgotten or places
never left, like

incalculable acceptance
of looking up—

and yet who is
looking from me

Seeking Clarity Amid Change

An experiential camera
can notice the waves

but not the depth of their source

I will permeate
the river's languish—
if there is current

I will wait for warmth

As my relics sit
in cabinets of amber,
light bends upon curve

through lucid lens

And the billowing past
stretches across stone,
cold distilled into negation,

an inhabitable valley,
some other morning's
copper cumulus—

I will wait for warmth

I will swallow fog

I'm Hollow

Seeing gaps between dust
clouds, the reverence

expanding my theory
of four walls—

the pinched places

hands upon pleasures
and getting good

at letting the heaviest
fall away.

Ripples in halo
show me the entry of impact

its interdependence

and I nod along,
being and looking

at the same time,
across rivers

surrounded in forgetting.

Incremental

Four noble oceans,
inseparable
from the eight
epiphanous waves

and the ten
thousand years
of measuring history.

    *

Reverse knots let
connections loose,
as if music was the
general noise

when the
lesson ends.

All My Songs

Sore back
and shoulders,
neck bent, the
clenched chords
outpace my octaves.

A half turn
toward resonance,
half counter turn
toward dissonance.
My fingertips

calloused, fret-
pressed. A string
broken, sinew
snagged, but let's just
play around them

and take a full turn
toward pressing on
the bruise, picking
the dried skin—
trying to tune

a semi-hollow body.

So called inside
is a boundless

voice, a noise happening
without distinction,

a malleable moon
watching my orbit,

a funny thought of
who's in whose way

Ineffably Awake

After staring at the ceiling
maybe we can recover

maybe we can
base our understanding

on a mass more than the planet
on a height more than the climb.

Maybe we can hitch a ride back
in time, give a gift instead

an alternate wholeness—
the hand unfolds, the fist uncoils

the roots alchemize,
the anchors dissolve.

After shedding the husk,
breathless density

we can enter the cave
blow ochre

umber, carbon black.
Savor the world.

Bring a light
a diamond disincarnate

dwell on a transfiguration
a moment of going somewhere else.

Upward Impermanence

A coral complexity
bridges us to formlessness—

Empty vessel
where the voice

is distant,
fingers reach,

lenses contract,
the darkness doubles

    *

What if temples
were built for

forgiveness
and equanimity

commentaries on
coming back to stillness

Disown—
Build and disown

What I Remember

The long drive ends back at water,
after looking at the edges of each

other, after the residue of effort,
the starkness of thirst.

Looking now past the marine
glow, gulls wheeling

toward twilight, the delicate
weight of their dilution resting

with the cliff, I can see its unbearable
face. Verticality precedes doubt,

precedes spiraling, my
reeling into night.

The gulls gone, flights of
self-protection to some

unscalable steepness, leaving me
gazing now into what's left—

And the leveling momentum
of it all, parked after the miles

there and back, the
noise and need

of silence, need of flight,
perpetually undiluted.

Cliffs sinking into shore,
laying plain the rock and wave,

the exposure of elements,
edges still there, clashing—

Contact and erasure, grace
and becoming's hush.

Unconditional Air

The slenderest branches
seek lunar light,

an imageless bequest
of impalpable rifts

suspended in wind,

daring with the
clarity of invention.

Two Winds

Like a moth
grief blinks

in thin air
almost empty

some landing
spot seen

only through
separation

Like droplets
upon leaves

longing rests
and release awaits

the mossy mass
buoyant in being

an ongoing hum
of exchange after rain

Self-Absorption

On balance, dense
and rare, looking
at leaves,

fungi folds upon bark,

gold shines through
the late October
limbs, the synapses

of redundancy.

Yellow light dims
through black branches.
Reactions against

the ordinariness

of knowing.
On boundless microbes,
everything became

meaningful;

in one act of forgiveness,
moss upon the loam
and ferns upstream

clearly layered

in the holiest shade,
in the low and dusk-
facing ground

newly awakened.

Our worldly winds,
ungovernable change:

A window cracked—
too cold
A window closed—
too hot

The residue
upon stuck sills

Ministry of Trust

Bitter milk seeps
to poison roots,
once willing;
sharp winds cross
the hardened dirt—

know everything
and let them in.

Clouds compress
into storm;
the blow is both
the resistance
and the invitation
to wait it out—

Soft feet sink
in soft ground;
a leaf on skin,
stalks brush up
ground to hand—

know everything
let them in.

To Feel Better

You take in
two August moons
just to let in something else's
                              orbit

the circle's apprentice above
and within a pulse
of somewhere else's
                        silence

                              its splinters

                                            its spectres

You make out edges of tree trunks
reflecting what they can
in limited light, but still
                                  a presence

                              a gloaming

                    is unquestionable

You take in another
indulgent August
just to be clothed in someone else's
                                          belonging

Jade

The coincidence of
rain on car roof

a self-surprising
arrangement

of form and water
falling into

each other and
just now made audible.

I recall the past pop
of some cork

a new year—
not this one

an apparition of stasis
like jade statues

on a distant shelf
not seen or sold

or given away.
Like the fool who

persists in folly,
I look for the cypress

tree every time
I drive by it.

When the highway curls
between park and cemetery,

the leaves add more
wet ink with each pass.

An improvised ritual—
bowl of water,

some foliage,
stones now named.

Challenges and
resources co-emerge

on the way home.

Coda

To cultivate distance
between dreams

and the candlelit
arrangement

of mistakes,
to walk by as if

they are the curbed
furniture, to sit

with the being-
ness of the unroomed

couch, the mattress
on gravel, the table

upended for stability
when gusts come, to bless

the ground upon which
our bared breaking rests.

The Half Turn

It takes a spacious blue
patience

to turn Saint Lucy's
flicker

into blazingly
radiant waves.

I can feel the warm air now,
the cool sea and hot stone

both soft and smooth
in my hands.

I look for the solstice,
wonder if there will be

more heat to place
upon this warming day,

bluer and more gentle
crests to come.

But one day's waiting won't
reveal that day's secret

or build cathedrals
to forgotten saints

or melt in sun
a frozen beach.

And yet somehow time pries
nails out of floorboards

and warps windows
and buckles the crossbeams;

it brings clear water
to a palm, points to a head,

then to a heart. There's no unburn
or unflame or unspark—

only a return to light, a practice
of happening.

The crack of expansion,

an oyster shell broken

open

About the Author

Aaron Lelito is a visual artist and writer from Buffalo, NY. He primarily draws inspiration from the patterns and imagery of nature, as well as one's personal, subjective relationship with the natural world. His images have been published as cover art in *Red Rock Review, Peatsmoke Journal,* and *The Scriblerus*. His work has also appeared in *Barzakh Magazine, Novus Literary Arts Journal, SPECTRA Poets, The Primer,* and *EcoTheo Review*. He is editor-in-chief of the art & literature website *Wild Roof Journal.*

www.ingramcontent.com/pod-product-compliance
Lightning Source LLC
Chambersburg PA
CBHW030916170426
43193CB00009BA/874